ULTIMATE CARS

Porsche

Rob Scott Colson

PowerKiDS press.

New York

Published in 2011 by The Rosen Publishing Group Inc.
29 East 21st Street, New York, NY 10010

First Edition

Editor: Camilla Lloyd
Produced by Tall Tree Ltd
Editor, Tall Tree: Emma Marriott
Designer: Jonathan Vipond

Library of Congress Cataloging-in-Publication Data

Colson, Rob Scott.
  Porsche / by Rob Scott Colson. -- 1st ed.
      p. cm. -- (Ultimate cars)
  Includes bibliographical references and index.
  ISBN 978-1-61532-623-5 (library binding)
  ISBN 978-1-61532-633-4 (paperback)
  ISBN 978-1-61532-634-1 (6-pack)
  1. Porsche automobile--Juvenile literature. I. Title.
  TL215.P75C64 2011
  629.222--dc22

                                             2009045428

Photographs
All images Dr. Ing. h.c. F. Porsche AG, except:
17t Lothar Spurzem/ Creative Commons
18 KS_Autosport / Alamy
19t Brian Snelson/ Creative Commons

Manufactured in China

CPSIA Compliance Information: Batch #WAS0102PK: For Further Information
contact Rosen Publishing, New York, New York at 1-800-237-9932

Contents

Porsche

In 1945, Austrian car designer Ferry Porsche was looking to buy a car. When he couldn't find what he wanted, Porsche decided to build it himself.

The result was the Porsche 356, which was first produced in 1948. The Porsche company has made luxury sports cars ever since. They also make cars for rallies—races with many stages run over several days—and endurance races, in which cars drive as far as they can in a set number of hours.

Amazing Designers

The Porsche company has always been a family business. Ferry Porsche (1909–98) is pictured here in 1968, sitting on his most famous car, the Porsche 911. He took over the family company when his father died in 1951, and remained in charge until his retirement in 1989. Porsche's son, Ferdinand, helped to design the 911, and his nephew, yet another Ferdinand, still part-owns the company.

Father and Son

The Porsche car design company was founded in 1931 by Ferry Porsche's father, Ferdinand. Father and son worked together in the 1930s to design the Volkswagen Beetle, one of the most popular cars ever created. Production continued until 2003, by which time over 21 million had been made.

This is the one millionth Beetle, built in 1955. Glass beads in the shiny chrome parts make it sparkle in the light.

Vintage cars drive past the distinctive cone-shaped Porsche building in Leipzig, Germany.

911 Carrera

The 911 is a 2-seater sports car that was first made in 1963.

The car has been updated several times since then—the 911 Carrera 4S Coupé pictured here went on sale in 2008. Versions of the 911 have competed in many different kinds of motorsports, winning races all over the world.

The 911 Carrera's Dynamic Bending Lights help the driver to see around corners at night. The lights point to the left as the driver turns the steering wheel left, lighting up the bending road ahead as the car changes direction.

Rear Engine

The engine of the 911 is at the back. This gives it a distinctive shape, with a high rear and low bonnet. The Coupé has a hard roof that cannot be removed. There is also a soft-top version of the 911, known as a Cabriolet, with a removable roof. Drivers who want the highest performance (the best acceleration and fastest speeds) choose the Coupé. The hard roof gives the car more strength, allowing it to accelerate from 0 to 62 miles per hour (0 to 100 kph) in 4.5 seconds—0.2 seconds faster than the Cabriolet.

Amazing Design

Before the driver can change gear, the engine must be disconnected from the wheels using the clutch. In most cars, this leads to a temporary loss of power. The 911 has two clutches—one for odd-numbered gears and another for even-numbered gears. The driver changes gear by disconnecting one clutch and instantly connecting to the other, meaning that there is no loss of power.

The gearshift moves from clutch to clutch and changes gear.

STATS AND FACTS

YEARS OF PRODUCTION **2008–present**

ENGINE SIZE **3.8 liter**

NUMBER OF CYLINDERS **6**

TRANSMISSION **Double-clutch**

GEARBOX **7-speed**

0–62 MPH (0–100 KPH) **4.5 seconds**

TOP SPEED **183 mph (295 kph)**

WEIGHT **3,450 lb. (1,565 kg)**

CO_2 EMISSIONS (G/KM) **251**

FUEL ECONOMY **26.4 mpg (10.7 L/100 km)**

Boxster

The Boxster is a 2-seater, open-top sports car. Its name is a combination of the words roadster and boxer. A roadster is a car with a removable roof.

The word "boxer" refers to the car's distinctive engine. The pistons, which pump up and down to produce the engine's power, are lined up in pairs facing each other, so that they meet in the middle, like two boxers touching gloves at the start of a fight.

STATS AND FACTS

YEARS OF PRODUCTION **2007–present**
ENGINE SIZE **2.7 liter**
NUMBER OF CYLINDERS **6**
TRANSMISSION **Manual (Stick shift)**
GEARBOX **6-speed**
0–62 MPH (0–100 KPH) **6.1 seconds**
TOP SPEED **162 mph (260 kph)**
WEIGHT **2,877 lb. (1,305 kg)**
CO_2 EMISSIONS (G/KM) **227**
FUEL ECONOMY **29.7 mpg (9.5 L/100 km)**

The 2007 987 model has prominent side intake vents, wheels up to 19 inches in diameter, and similar-profile headlights to the Carrera GT.

Amazing Design

The bar at the back of the car is known as a spoiler. It lies flat against the car's body at low speeds. This allows air to flow smoothly over the car. At higher speeds, the spoiler moves up and disrupts, or spoils, the air flow. This slows the car, but it also produces downforce, which pushes down on the wheels and makes sure that they grip the road safely.

The spoiler automatically rises up when the Boxster's speed reaches 75 mph (120 kph), and goes down again when it slows to 50 mph (80 kph).

The soft top can be opened or closed in just 12 seconds.

Retracting Roof

At the press of a button, the soft roof folds back electronically into a space behind the seats. It can be opened or closed in just 12 seconds while driving at speeds of up to 31 mph (50 kph). The Boxster is also available with a removable aluminum hard top, which has a heated rear window. It cannot be put back on while driving, so the driver and passenger will get wet in an unexpected rain shower.

Cayman S

The Cayman is a 2-seater, named after a crocodilelike reptile that may be small but can give a nasty bite.

Every part of the Cayman has been fine-tuned for maximum performance. To prove its speed, Porsche tested it at Germany's famous Nürburgring race track, where it lapped in 8 minutes 20 seconds—almost as fast as the more powerful 911 Carrera.

STATS AND FACTS

YEARS OF PRODUCTION **2006–present**
ENGINE SIZE **3.4 liter**
NUMBER OF CYLINDERS **6**
TRANSMISSION **Manual (Stick shift)**
GEARBOX **6-speed**
0–62 MPH (0–100 KPH) **5.4 seconds**
TOP SPEED **171 mph (275 kph)**
WEIGHT **2,954 lb. (1,340 kg)**
CO_2 EMISSIONS (G/KM) **254**
FUEL ECONOMY **26.6 mpg (10.6 L/100 km)**

Suspension

The wheels of a car are connected to the chassis (the car's skeleton) using springs and shock absorbers. This is known as the suspension. A soft suspension gives the car's occupants the most comfortable ride, but reduces performance. The Cayman has 2 suspension settings—soft for longer-distance comfort, or stiff to give your Cayman an even nastier bite.

Amazing Design

The driver can find out all kinds of information about the car's performance using the on-board computer. The Porsche Sports Chrono system includes a stopwatch that tells the driver how they are performing down to the last hundredth of a second. A Cayman S with Sports Chrono lapped the Nürburgring circuit 3 seconds faster than the same car without it.

Sports Chrono stopwatch

Cayenne GTS

The Cayenne is a very different car from other Porsches. It is big, with 4 doors and room inside for 5 adults. This is an SUV (a sport utility vehicle).

The Cayenne is a 4-wheel drive, which means that the engine is connected to all the wheels, and it is as happy driving over rough ground or through mud as it is on a road.

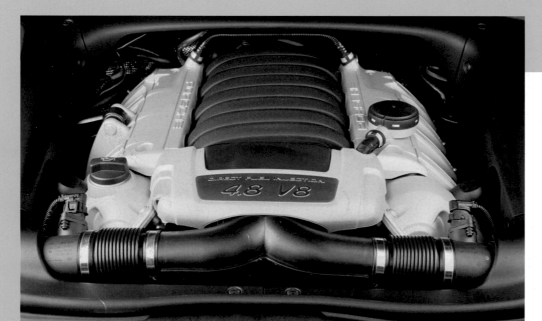

The Cayenne's large 4.8-liter V8 engine works with a direct fuel-injection system. This gives the driver a smoother engine response and a more reliable start.

STATS AND FACTS

YEARS OF PRODUCTION 2002–present
ENGINE SIZE 4.8 liter
NUMBER OF CYLINDERS 8
TRANSMISSION Manual (Stick shift)
GEARBOX 6-speed
0–62 MPH (0–100 KPH) 6.1 seconds
TOP SPEED 157 mph (253 kph)
WEIGHT 4,905 lb. (2,225 kg)
CO₂ EMISSIONS (G/KM) 361
FUEL ECONOMY 18.7 mpg (15.1 L/100 km)

Amazing Design

The Cayenne's engine is made more powerful by direct fuel injection. Fuel is usually mixed with air before entering the cylinders. In normal engines, this is done in a chamber just outside the cylinders. In the Cayenne, fuel is injected directly into the cylinder and the air enters separately. This allows the car's computer to time the fuel injection and make sure that all the fuel burns correctly.

The high-resolution screen displays GPS (Global Positioning System), maps, and other information.

New Technology

There are no signs to tell you which way to go when you drive off-road. But the driver of the Cayenne can find out using its Communication Management System. By sending a signal to satellites in space, the car's computer can figure out exactly where you are.

The GTS is the first in the Cayenne series to feature a combination of steel springs and PASM, a high-tech suspension system.

356

Ferry Porsche's very first car was a lightweight, easy-to-handle sports car—exactly the car Porsche himself wanted to drive.

He soon found that lots of other people wanted to drive one, too, and a total of 76,000 were made. Many different models were produced, including coupés and roadsters (also called convertibles), with engines ranging in size from 1.1 to 2 liters. They were all stylish, high-performance, 2-seater cars.

This is a 356 B Roadster from 1960. By the 1960s, 356 engines were producing over 100 horsepower.

Amazing Design

The 356 squeezed all the power it could from its small 4-cylinder engine. The first models used a Volkswagen engine similar to the one that powered the Beetle. With its finely tuned suspension and light weight, the 356 produced much more power than the Beetle. Power is measured in units called horsepower or hp. The Beetle produced 25 hp, and the first 356 produced 40 hp.

engine in the rear

steering column connects the steering wheel to the front wheels

suspension

Hard Top

This coupé version (below) of the 356 was made in 1962. It was powered by a larger 6-cylinder engine, and had a top speed of 115 mph (185 kph). It was one of the last 356 models to be made. By 1963, Porsche were also making the more powerful 911, and production of the 356 ended two years later.

STATS AND FACTS

YEARS OF PRODUCTION **1948–65 (this model 1960)**
ENGINE SIZE **1.6 liter**
NUMBER OF CYLINDERS **4**
TRANSMISSION **Manual (Stick shift)**
GEARBOX **4-speed**
0–62 MPH (0–100 KPH) **10 seconds**
TOP SPEED **112 mph (180 kph)**
WEIGHT **3,748–5,062 lb. (1,700–2,296 kg) (range of all models)**
CO_2 EMISSIONS (G/KM) **Not available**
FUEL ECONOMY **30 mpg (9.4 L/100 km)**

Le Mans

The 24-Hour Le Mans is the ultimate test for an endurance car. Teams of drivers take turns to drive around a 8.5 mile (13.6 km) circuit in the French town of Le Mans.

The car that has completed the most circuits after 24 hours of continuous racing is the winner. Fuel economy, durability, and the drivers' ability to concentrate over long periods are just as important as raw speed at Le Mans.

The modified 962 reclaims victory at the 1994 Le Mans.

STATS AND FACTS

962
YEARS OF PRODUCTION **1994**
ENGINE SIZE **3 liter**
NUMBER OF CYLINDERS **6**
TRANSMISSION **Automatic**
GEARBOX **5-speed**
0–62 MPH (0–100 KPH) **2.7 seconds**
TOP SPEED **249 mph (401 kph)**
WEIGHT **2,271 lb. (1,030 kg)**
CO_2 EMISSIONS (G/KM)
Not available
FUEL ECONOMY
Not available

Race to Win

Porsche won Le Mans seven years in a row from 1981 to 1987. But new rules that required competing cars to be more like legal road cars ended Porsche's dominance. They won again in 1994 when they teamed up with the German company Dauer to modify the 962 with a longer tail, larger fuel tank, and narrower tires.

Actor Steve McQueen drove a Porsche 908 like this one in the film Le Mans, *which charted his progress in the 1970 race.*

The Rules

Each Le Mans is really four races in one, with four different classes of car competing. There are two classes for purpose-built cars, such as the Porsche 962, and two more classes for ordinary production cars. Each class has different rules for minimum weight and a specified fuel allowance to last the race.

Cars of many shapes and sizes compete at Le Mans. At the 1951 race pictured here, the Porsche 356 won its class for production cars.

956

The 956 was designed to compete in endurance races. It could reach 249 mph (400 kph) on the 3.7 mile (6 km) Mulsanne Straight at Le Mans.

In addition to speed, endurance cars also need to be extremely reliable, and the 956 could keep going for many hours, with only the occasional pit stop to take on fuel and change driver and tires.

Amazing Design

In an ordinary car, the chassis is made of two layers: a frame on the inside that gives it its strength, with another layer (the skin) on the outside. The chassis of the 956 is a monocoque (French for "one shell"), which means that it is made from one layer. The monocoque chassis is much stronger, allowing the car to go at high speeds for longer.

STATS AND FACTS

YEARS OF PRODUCTION **1982–84**
ENGINE SIZE **2.65 liter**
NUMBER OF CYLINDERS **6**
TRANSMISSION **Manual (Stick shift)**
GEARBOX **5-speed**
0–62 MPH (0–100 KPH) **3.4 seconds**
TOP SPEED **Over 217 mph (350 kph)**
WEIGHT **1,608 lb. (820 kg)**
CO_2 EMISSIONS (G/KM) **Not available**
FUEL ECONOMY
Not available

The huge, winglike spoiler at the back stops the car from taking off at top speed by using air resistance to force it down onto the track.

Winning Car

The 956 first appeared at the 24-Hour Le Mans race in 1982. Porsche entered three 956s, and they finished first, second, and third. Porsche totally dominated the race, with their older car, the 935, coming in fourth and fifth. Pictured below is the winning car, which was driven by the team of Belgian Jacky Ickx and Briton Derek Bell.

959

The Porsche 959 was the most advanced car of its time to be allowed on the road. Two hundred were sold to the public, but this was really a car made to race.

The 959 was one of the first high-performance cars with 4-wheel drive. This meant that it was durable and fast—perfect for off-road rallies and driving on rough ground.

Rally Driving

In 1986, the Porsche 959 was entered in the Paris–Dakar Rally. This grueling race is the ultimate challenge for rally drivers. Over three weeks, the competitors drove 3,107 miles (6,000 km) from Paris, France, to Dakar, Senegal, crossing the Sahara Desert. The car's French drivers, René Metge and Dominique Lemoyne, won the rally in their new car.

STATS AND FACTS

Years of production **1986–89**
Engine size **2.85 liter**
Number of cylinders **6**
Transmission **Manual (Stick shift)**
Gearbox **6-speed**
0–62 mph (0–100 kph) **3.7 seconds**
Top speed **186 mph (300 kph)**
Weight **3,197 lb. (1,450 kg)**
CO_2 Emissions (g/km) **Not available**
Fuel economy
13 mpg (21.7 L/100 km)

suspension

drivetrain

engine

Amazing Design

From the outside, the 959 looks very similar to a 911. But looks can be deceptive. The 911's body is made mostly of steel, but the only metal parts of the 959's body are the hood and door panels. The rest is made of plastic! This is nothing like the plastic a toy car is made from. It is a special material called Kevlar, which is so strong it is used to make bulletproof armor.

Glossary

chassis
The frame of the car to which the body and engine are attached.

clutch
A means of disconnecting the engine from the wheels in order to change gear.

coupé
A car with a hard roof that cannot be removed.

cylinder
A chamber in an engine inside which pistons pump up and down.

drivetrain
A metal shaft that connects the gearbox to the axles that drive the wheels.

endurance race
A race in which cars are driven as far as they can within a set time limit.

fuel economy
The rate at which a car uses fuel. It is measured in miles per gallon (mpg) or liters per 100 kilometers (L/100 km).

gear
A system of cogs that controls the transfer of power from the engine to the wheels. Low gears give extra power for acceleration and high gears are used for faster speeds.

horsepower (hp)
A unit of measurement for a car's power.

performance
A measurement of a car's power. A car that accelerates quickly and has a high top speed is said to be high performance.

piston
A cylindrical metal rod that pumps up and down inside a cylinder to produce an engine's power.

production car
A car that is usually made in large numbers and is offered for sale to the public.

rally
A car race that takes place in stages over several days, often on rough off-road ground.

roadster
A 2-seater car with a removable roof, also called a convertible.

spoiler
A bar at the back of a car that interrupts the flow of air over the car, producing downforce that stops the car from leaving the road at high speeds or around corners.

sport utility vehicle (SUV)
A powerful and strong 4-wheel-drive car designed to be driven off-road.

suspension
A system of springs and shock absorbers that makes the ride smoother as the wheels pass over bumps.

Models at a Glance

Model	Years Made	Numbers Built	Did You Know?
356	1948–65	76,000	As a highly regarded collector car, a fully restored 356 Carrera Speedster will sell for around $350,000.
997 series (including the current 911 Carrera)	2004–present	100,000	The 997 is the most commercially successful 911 of all time. Between 2004 and 2007, 100,000 were sold.
Boxster	1996–present (latest model produced in 2007)	17,519 in 2008	The 987 Boxster shares only 20% of its components with its predecessor, despite looking almost identical.
Cayman	2006–present	10,000 per year	The Cayman is named after a crocodilelike reptile, also called a caiman.
Cayenne	2002–present	40,000 per year	The Cayenne is the first V8-engined car built by Porsche since 1995.
956	1982–84	28	In 1985, Stefan Bellof died while racing a 956 after colliding with Jacky Ickx's newer 962.
959	1986–89	337	During its lifetime, the 959 had only one competitor with comparable performance—the Ferrari F40.

Further Reading

Blazers: Porsche
by Lisa Bullard
(Capstone Press, 2007)

Porsche: The Engineering Story
by Jeff Daniels
(Haynes Publishing, 2008)

Porsche: The Road From Zuffenhausen
by Dennis Adler
(Random House, 2003)

Web Sites

Due to the changing nature of Internet links, PowerKids Press has developed an online list of Web sites related to the subject of this book. This site is updated regularly. Please use this link to access this list:
http://www.powerkidslinks.com/uc/porsche

Index

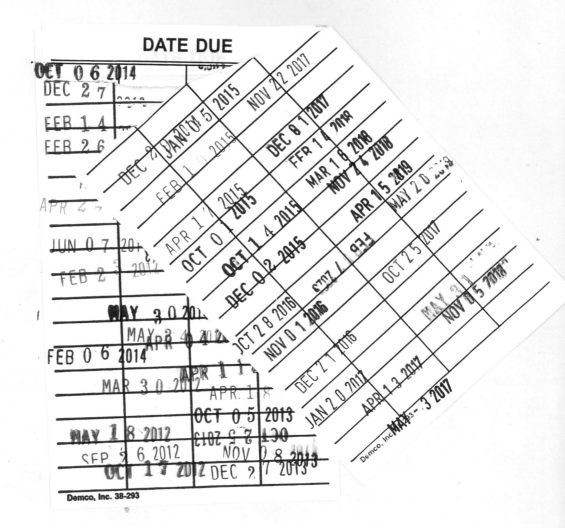

DATE DUE